My Poems are Yours

The Poetic Soliloquies of Hope and Courage

Jenevieve (Peach) Woods
with
Pete Geissler

The Expressive Press
www.TheExpressivePress.com
info@theexpressivepress.com

ISBN-13: 978-1545359501
ISBN-10: 1545359504

Other books by the Author

- Peach

Related Books from The Expressive Press

- The Power of Ethics
- The Power of Dignity
- The Power of Being Articulate
- The Power of Writing Well

Cover Photo by: JeffGeissler.com
Cover Design by: Samiha Nawshin

TABLE OF CONTENTS

PROLOGUE:
On Poetry; On Peach's Poetry
Observations from her publisher

Voltaire, the pseudonym of François-Marie Arouet (born November 21, 1694, Paris, France — died May 30, 1778, Paris) is one of the greatest of all French writers. He said that *Poetry is the music of the soul; and, above all, of great and feeling souls.*

Peach, the pseudonym of Jenevieve Woods, is one of those rare writers who fearlessly and eagerly bares her soul, not only in her poetry, but also in her prose and life. She writes with rigorous honesty, unflagging authenticity, and boundless optimism.

Readers of this collection will be rewarded with a deeply moving view and understanding of a soul that is battling the adversity of a genetic condition — mitochondrial disease — that has certainly altered the course of her life, but also could shorten it. She has turned her condition into an opportunity to change the way the rest of us think about equality, inclusion, courage, hope. She has turned her condition into a celebration of herself and of life. She offers us her gift of dreams and a reassurance for a brighter future that respects tolerance, joy, love, and dignity, and that eschews despair.

I first met Peach in May of 2016. Since then, we have collaborated to publish her autobiography, *PEACH: An Exceptional Teen's Inspiring Journey for Universal Acceptance*. Readers' laudatory and heartfelt responses to several of her poems in that book prompted us to publish this collection, which I predict will be a moveable feast of new editions.

I also predict with the confidence of experience that, after reading this short but compelling book, you will love Peach, as I do, in her own right, comfortable in her own deteriorating body, comfortable with her surroundings, comfortable with her role in bettering the world.

Pete Geissler,
Founder, The Expressive Press

1. ON MITOCHONDRIAL DISEASE

The Good, the Terrible, the Enigma

Mito is a word for life
It is the energy within all cells
Energy we need for life
Energy we need for living.

My energy is damaged
Like a lamp with no electricity
No plug and no way to shine
I feel like my plug is damaged

No matter how much electrical tape I put on
It still fails

The medications
Doctors
And
Life
Encourage me to shine

I am trying
To shine

*

The study, the study, the study

Scary
But necessary
Will it save me
I will save you
I try to think it will

I want to save everyone
The drug makes me sick
It makes me weak
But I hope it makes me strong

All the prodding poking and the alike
It hurts
But I close my eyes
Clinch my fist

And pray the pain away

***

2. ON CELEBRATING ME

I Love My Brain; I love Yours, Too

To my brain
I am glad you are mine
I see the world in a different way
It's not prom dresses and life
It is people and heart that I see
I am glad that you are mine

You are smart
And you help me live
But we need to talk about this fog
In the morning; it's like smog
I jump out of bed like a frog
I need time to deal with the smoke
For at times my brain really can choke

I still love your shine
When you are on you're mine
When the fog comes we giggle
I can't do much else when it comes

Not sure where the laughing comes from
My mom yells, are you ok
Yes, just laughing the day away

*

You are one decision away
From a totally new life
I heard that today
And my decision is to fight

I want to be in sight
So get ready
I have a lot to say
I feel amazing today

*

A cupcake today
To celebrate
Nothing in particular
An ordinary day

I celebrate me today
In a special way
Just me and the cupcake
It's yummy
And sweet
And I think that it is neat

To sit a bit
And just be me

*

Looking deep
I think it is neat

To climb the steep
Mountain
My goal
Is large
And I am in charge
Of my life

I am choosing life
And love
And strife
For I need to accomplish this goal
So I can unfold my soul

The pain inside
Leaks sometimes
But as a whole
I am ready

To talk and walk steady
To impact the many
To love
Each other

***

3. ON SUPPORT

*The Awesome Power of my Heroes: Mom, Family,
and Friends*

Mom is a lame word
That everyone calls their creator
Words like warrior, hero
And slayer of Darth Vader

This fits my creator much more
She is my life and helps me soar
I could go on and on about how much she means
Thank you for everything you 're one in a million

For never giving up and giving in
For being a woman of distinction
That I aspire to be
Oh my mom how much I love thee

*

When I die I have a question
Why
Why did I have to be the one
Who had no fun in the sun

Why can't I fly like the rest
To be my best
My mom is an angel
Always there waiting for me

I don't know why she doesn't see
How awful it can be
She is my world
And maybe that's the gift

I see many girls
Throw fits
With their mom

I don't want to break away
I want things to stay this way

*

Heroes are amazing
Both big and small
They impact every part of me
And because of them I feel more free

Thank you, Susan, Dave and Pete alike
For believing I am worth all my might
To Ricky and men, contractors and friends
Living this life because of your amends

Thank you, Mike, and Joe and Steven
Because of you my life feels even.
You gave me a candle when all was dark
Because of you I feel a spark

Your gift to me
Just so you know
To continue to fight
And grow

I will never forget what you did for me
I will remember the people who set me free.

*

I missed you today
I hate it when you go away
Because you are always with me

I know you want a life
But I struggle without you
Peach you said please understand

No matter where I am
I am your biggest fan!

Mom needs some time
But you are fused inside
And I am very proud of you
And I am always with you

*

What are you thinking?

I see you with my mom and I love it
She laughs and my heart sings
My life has been enriched because of you

13

And I am concerned

That you will eventually be through with us
Will it be too much?
I hope not
For you have become
A man I can depend on
And confide in

I love you

*

Thinking about happy
A few themes emerge

I love dogs
I love people
I love food
I love tea
I love you

All of you
Even the mean you
I think about who you are
Someday you will come
Who are you?
I think about you
My special someone
I am waiting for you

*

I saw your eyes today

The sadness cuts me
I am sorry Mommy

If I had my wings
Would it be better
I could watch you and save you from the weather
I would sprinkle you with love and kindness alike

But sometimes I think
When you look at me
I think I give you what you need

I know I am a source of your pain
But I also love you insane
Mommy you give me light in the rain
And life

I want to give it back
And I would sacrifice myself and more

To see you soar

*

Austere in stature
Masterful and playful
Describes you best
An admiration grew
A mentor
A friend

Pete, you are to me
The man who set me free
From myself

Confidence built
Relationship created

Admiration grew
Who ever knew my crush would be you
(Just kidding Abby)

Through this journey I have felt
A need to grow and melt
Into a new
I am learning to be
As much as I can

Thank you for being part of my plan
I hope to do more
And come to your door
For there I feel free
To be ME!

*

Lady in Red
Advocates for me
I am glad to see
And have grown so fond of thee

I appreciate your thoughts
Your time
Your patience
With me

I enjoy the time
When we talk I thrive
For you listen and respond

With elegance

With you I grow
And begin to know
Your kindness does show
Thank you again
For being my friend

*

The Coach

The believer in me
Everyone needs one
I have one
And it's not the one you think

I speak of mom
And Mark alike
But this is my coach
My spark my light

He was a stranger
To me
But the kindness I did see
His eyes are kind
A little bit deep

I see I see
Someone so kind
I laugh as he speaks so eloquently
of wine
A laugh

A joke
A clearing of his throat

Back to my coach
With tasks to do
Things he wants me to do
I am eager to learn
And when he smiles and laughs
I know it's just Pete

Pete, you are neat
From your head to your feet.

***

4. ON BEING INVISIBLE

It's as awful as much as it's unnecessary

I am the INVISIBLE GIRL...
I am here but you don't see me
I am here but you don't think about me
I am here but you don't care about me

There are times I say hi
But you walk by
There are times when I cry
But you don't care

BTW, the other day when I fell, you all walked over me
That hurt
And when my bag fell down the steps and you kicked it
That hurt too

I know what I would do if I could
I would help
Hold out my hand
And ask, "Are you ok?"

It doesn't take that much
To be human
I want to remind you, that although I have a disability

I am a person

I was not given the gifts you have been given
But I have something you don't
I see people as people
And celebrate your life
A life I will never have

You see me as damaged
And that is sad
And yes, these words are hard
Because my days at North Hills High are just like this
You ask why?

Well let me enlighten you,
Yes, I have a disease
it is called Mitochondrial Disease
Yes, I can't walk real well
Yes, my vision is fading
I ask the only person I have, my mom

WHY?

She inspires me to try and reminds me of my many gifts
"Inspire them Peach," she says…
So… although it may be hard I have something to say…
If you took just a second you would see that …

I have many gifts
I am smart
I am kind
I will continue to achieve

For me there is no option
Let my words inside you
Let the change begin!

*

Laughed at and mocked
Tripped and torn
As I sat thinking
I began to feel a ball inside
Grow to hot
Then to nothing

This ball was a friend
A confidant
A way to understand those who smite me
I feel invisible

I wished I had never been born
Never been able to be abused OR IGNORED
At this moment – a choice
To grow or wither
To forgive and forget

And make a difference
I, Jenevieve choose to heal
I choose to fly
I choose to accept
I choose to love
I choose to impact
I choose to celebrate differences

And I will until
I am stopped by death…

21

*

Living a life I didn't ask for
Can be an interesting task

I dream of walking running and playing
Instead I have to stay
In my world

People don't see
They judge instead
I am just me

*

Today is a dream
I was able to be seen
The people were listening
To me
I feel free
To live
My way

*

What do you see
When you see me
Do you see broken?

I am broken but in the broken is beauty
A cracked view of me
In the shards' of glass a sparkle
Of dancing and marvel

22

Maybe one day when you look
You will see inside the broken glass
Is beautiful me

*

A cake in my face
I saw you as you tripped her
She fell onto the floor
And the café all laughed

Why?
What was its worth?
Are you a hero
I wish I was an ant

And could crawl deep inside
Your head and talk some sense
Into you

But for now all I can do
Is watch
The cake splattered all over me
And my face

I got up to help but security got there first
I never saw that girl again
Why did you need to do that?

***

5. ON THE AMAZING STRENGTH OF FAITH AND HOPE

I Cannot Live Without it; Can You?

I have faith in life
Faith in love
Faith in hope
Faith in people

I have faith that my life will work
Faith that I will keep talking
Faith that I will keep walking
Faith that I will going
Faith that someday
Someone will love me

Faith that I can be free

*

People say hope floats
What does that mean
It can't be readily seen
It can be acted
And reacted
Among people

Who believe
I believe in hope
And I understand now how it floats

For I have big hopes
That I am able to live
Happy and free

And simply be me

***

6. ON FRIENDS

The Real, the Pretenders

Friend is a word I don't understand
This is forging to me in this land
Friend means kindness and love
And I have only been shoved
Into a cube

Stay in your lane
I say inside
You are not worth the friendship by wise
So I stay alone in my place in my head

And maybe someday friend will mean more
But for now it can't store
Any memories of love, life or laughter

*

We are not friends

Killing them with kindness is what I do
You walked over me
I counted your shoes
One, two , three, eighteen

Never reached out
To see what was wrong
I need to forget about
How I felt

I laid there a bit and wondered a lot
How I really got into this spot
This point I turned
As I sat there and squirmed
I am really sad
But also glad

I know we are not friends
I am motivated to change
And the thought remains

Why?

***

7. ON CHANGING THE DIALOGUE

It's a Start

Can't
Can't
Can't
That is a four letter word

People become upset about cussing
And I say that they are fussing
About the wrong word
If you want to know what's wrong with the world start with
the word CAN'T

Can't means you won't
Can't is why you don't
And how do you know if you can if you always say can't
Can't would be my death

Dig me a hole and place me inside
For all I could do is stay and hide.
I have an idea
Try can
You can do what you put your mind to

I am sure you can

For I do everyday
It's my master plan
To show you

*

I watch and I learn
I try hard
But I do get angry
Mad even

I can't
No Jenna
Don't give into the bullies
It's not you
It is hard at times

And I wish
That it was not
TRUE
I wish
I wish
I wish

And for now that is all I can do

*

Make lemonade
People say to make lemonade from lemons when things get
ruff

Things are ruff and they are tuff
But I decided to do my best

And make lemon water instead

Lemonade is yummy
But is sugar and tart
Where lemon water is
Full of good stuff

I want to be pure
Of heart and spirt
Because in life
It's the actions that matter more than the voice

So drink and be healthy
Tomorrow is another day
Don't wish it away

*

I observed a turtle the other day
Safe inside his shell he did stay

Basking in the sun wishing the day away
As I watched the turtle head emerged
Looking around he began to submerged
Into the deep
He didn't want to creep
On the bank

Instead he decided and sank
To the bottom
As he journeyed to the bottom
I watched and saw

He was moving around

All safe and sound in the deep
He headed for the falls

He emerged on the bank wet
And his feet were set
In the sand
He didn't move an inch
And resting on his shell was a yellow finch
His head shut in as he clinched

And that is the way he stayed inside
He played

I wish I could hide
Inside for no one to see
To hide away for everyone but me
But that would be against my goals in life
To be seen and visible

So I bid you good day
And hope today you will come out and play

Your way!

***

8. ON BEAUTY AND LOVE
Inseparable Forever

Love
Someday I hope to know love
Love from a person who can see
That I am more
More than a stutter
More than a limp
More much more
I want to know love

*

Violets
Violets are beautiful
So fragrant and alive
I sit as I watch them blow and strive
They blow back and forth in the wind

I have been sitting on this bench watching them every year
Then one day they didn't appear
No one bothered to clean up the leaves
And now I can't see them dance
In the wind

Remember that to see beauty you may
Need to see
Through the leaves

I missed you today

*

Sunshine
Warm sun on this day
I am feeling blue today
Please don't go away
I need you today
The warmth feels like a hug
And I feel like a slug

Please go away
Soon
I have work to do
Books to read

Homework to do
Journals to write
So I will try with all my might
To heal

Sun stay with me today!

*

I saw something today
And it won't go away
It was a mom weeping in the hallway
Her baby was taken away

I wanted to hold her

But instead I walked over to her
And offered my hand
She reached out and squeezed me
I felt the wet

I felt for her
And all I did was sit
She got up and left
I think of her often

*

Why didn't you care
Why did you lie
You never wanted me
And you pretend now that you did

You are not fit
To be my creator
But I know now that it has to be this way
And I can say

That you are my donor but nothing more
I have much more in store
I have someone who loves me
And I can see what it means
That blood is really only one way
A true love is all I need

*

Today is beautiful
It can be for you
I am looking at the love in you
Let's make a pact

To love each other instead
I am a friend
That can live in your head
I will trust you and treat you with care

And no love will be spared

*

A flower
A flower is not more than a flower
But it is a flower
A beautiful gift

If you stop
Look
Listen
And
Maybe smell
You would be amazed at what you really see

Its beauty can be appreciated
What a wonderful world it would be
If we all treated each other like flowers

I want to be a sunflower

*

Orange is the new black
In fashion I find that interesting
But the color orange
Means life

It's juice
It's the sun
It's vitamins
It's fun
It's Fall

It's loving pie and candy
It's giving thanks with friends
And family
So orange to me is loving life

So if orange is the new black
I think it's great!

***

9. ON GOALS AND THE EPHEMERAL NATURE OF TIME

My New Beginning. Yours?

When people talk about goals
I have many
But mine are different
Legs today you have to work

I need you to understand
That I have to walk on this land
To be alive
I can use the chair

But we don't have a love affair
And I don't want to give in
I am strong
And I am capable
But I need you to work
So let's make a deal
if you work for me
I will soak you later,
I will make sure you are not blue
I will slap you back to pink
That's a promise

*

You are one decision away from a totally new life
I heard that today
And my decision is to fight
I want to be in sight
So get ready
I have a lot to say
I feel amazing today

*

Time
Time is a stealer
Takes things away
I want more
But I have to say

That it is what it is
And I hate saying that
God has put me on the mat
Time is a thief

And a criminal at that
I want my life
But it does not want me

*

Rules in life
Are taught in strife
We are taught to hate
And taught to love

When we are young we don't see difference
We only see friend
Someone you say you will be there until the end

When we grow
It does show
That we learn how
To hate....

We all know this inside
But it does not have to be our fate
It's never too late
To change.

What makes me craze
Is hearing that people can't change
When I know it's not true
Your days are not through

Be true
To yourself
And others
And remember this

Someone you hate
Is someone's baby
Would you want that fate for yours?

Communicate

Instead of hate
Accept
And relate

To what it must feel
To ignore your inner zeal

Use the energy for good
You know you should!
I am one standing for you

Please join me
And we can see it though
To a light
So bright

A world anew
Stand up for your fellow peeps
It's not that steep
Of a trek

Together
We can all change
And none of this is in vain

For a better world I see
With you and with me !
I am counting on you to see

How great and awesome it can be.

***

Made in the USA
Middletown, DE
03 October 2017